Animal Helpers

By Michele Spirn

Scott Foresman
is an imprint of

Glenview, Illinois • Boston, Massachusetts • Chandler, Arizona •
Upper Saddle River, New Jersey

Photographs

Every effort has been made to secure permission and provide appropriate credit for photographic material. The publisher deeply regrets any omission and pledges to correct errors called to its attention in subsequent editions.

Unless otherwise acknowledged, all photographs are the property of Pearson Education, Inc.

Photo locators denoted as follows: Top (T), Center (C), Bottom (B), Left (L), Right (R), Background (Bkgd)

Opener Fuse/Getty Images; **1** ©Melanie Stetson Freeman/The Christian Science Monitor/Getty Images; **3** (T) Altrendo Images/Getty Images; **4** (B) Bruno Morandi/ Getty Images; **5** William Thomas Cain/Getty Images; **6** ©Fancy/Veer/Corbis; **7** ©Melanie Stetson Freeman/The Christian Science Monitor/Getty Images; **8** Imagebroker/Alamy Images; **9** Bob Landry/Getty Images; **10** ©Bettmann/Corbis; **11** Maslov Dmitry/Fotolia; **12** Jupiter Images; **13** Frank Greenaway/©DK Images; **14** Peter Arnold, Inc./Alamy Images; **15** Fuse/Getty Images.

ISBN 13: 978-0-328-51642-1
ISBN 10:   0-328-51642-2

11 12 V0FL 16 15 14

Trained dogs can help blind people safely move about on busy streets.

There are many animals that help people. They are called service animals. These animals are not pets. They have important jobs to do. The animals have to be trained to do their jobs.

You may have seen people who are blind walking with guide dogs that were wearing harnesses. These dogs are service animals. They are trained to help their blind owners avoid dangerous situations. However, other animals are also helpful to people. Did you know that horses, monkeys, and even snakes can be helpers?

Horses Help People

Horses have helped people for thousands of years. Horses once **roamed** wild over **vast** parts of Asia. Then people learned they could tame them and ride them to travel farther than ever before. Horses could also carry heavy loads and help people in danger. For example, they could pull people out of a dangerous position such as getting stuck in **quicksand**.

Farmers use horses because they are strong animals. They can pull plows to help plant crops. They can also help people survive. For example, if crops were **infested** with pests and not safe to eat, horses could bring safe food from other places to people who needed it.

This nomadic couple rely on their horses to help them move all their belongings from one area in Mongolia to another.

4

Tiny horses can guide blind people just as guide dogs do.

Today, horses, especially small horses, have a new use. Instead of training only guide dogs, some people are now training small horses to help blind people. Like guide dogs, these horses can help people avoid things that might be dangerous, such as **rickety** steps. Horses can guide people safely across a street. They can even guide people around a supermarket.

Helping People with Disabilities

Animals such as cats and dogs have long been used to help people with disabilities. Having a pet for company can make a sick person feel better. Petting and playing with a cat or dog can also help people start moving around after an operation or a serious illness. Learning how to move again after a serious illness is very important to a person's health. These animals can help people make simple movements again, such as picking something up.

Cats can help stroke victims learn how to move again.

This monkey is trained to help paraplegics.

Monkey College

The monkey is another animal that can help people who can't move on their own. Monkeys can be trained to fetch remote controls, flip light switches, and open containers. There is even a special "monkey college" where they learn how to do these things.

One person uses her monkey to help her calm down when she gets upset. If she feels as if she is getting upset or angry, the monkey will pat her hair and give her hugs. The monkey will do this until she is calmer.

Dogs are also famous for rescuing people from dangerous situations. St. Bernard dogs are known for rescuing people who get lost in the cold and snowy Alps, a mountain range in Europe. When these dogs find a lost traveler, the person may be suffering from the extremely cold weather. The St. Bernard lies on top of the traveler and licks his or her face to warm and awaken him or her. Then the dog barks loudly to signal for help.

At a special school in Italy, rescue dogs are trained to save people from drowning. These dogs are taught to jump from helicopters to help people who are in trouble in the water.

St. Bernard dogs are famous for rescuing people in the Alps.

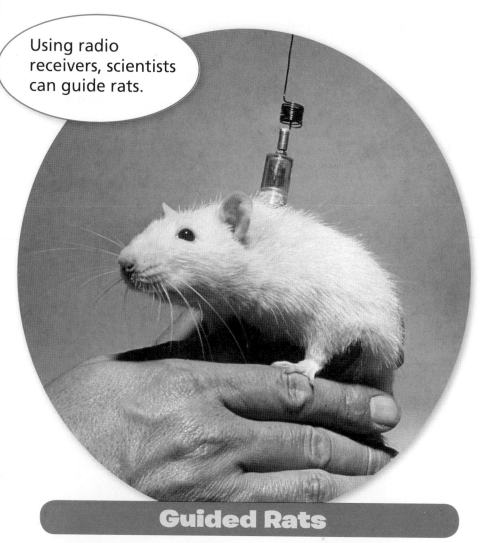

Using radio receivers, scientists can guide rats.

Guided Rats

Other animals are also learning useful things. Scientists with the **ambition** to see what rats could do strapped radio receivers to the animals' backs. When they sent radio signals to the receivers, the rats moved in the direction the scientists wanted. Perhaps in the future, guided rats will be able to find people trapped in **landslides** or root out things that are hidden from sight.

Pigeons in Wartime

Pigeons have long been used as messengers in times of war. People fighting against an enemy often wanted to be able to send important messages to friends and soldiers. They used specially trained pigeons called homing pigeons. These birds were fast and trustworthy. During some wars, pilots carried pigeons in their planes. If the pilots were in danger, they would release the birds. The birds flew with messages that said that the pilots needed help.

This pigeon is being used to send an important message out during wartime.

Our Coast Guard once believed that pigeons could be used to find shipwrecks and people lost at sea. Some pigeons have been trained to find objects in the sea. They have excellent vision and hearing. They've also been trained to tell helicopter pilots where to fly.

Pigeons can be trained to find things in the ocean.

Parrots

Even people who have trouble controlling their anger can be helped by animals. One man who couldn't stop his angry outbursts was given a parrot. This bird seemed to sense when the man was getting angry. The bird told him to calm down and it worked! Birds can help in other ways as well. They can help people who can't move by pushing buttons or fetching things.

Parrots and other birds can also be trained to help people.

Little Suckers

Animals can also help people in unusual ways. Hundreds of years ago, leeches–wormlike animals that suck blood–were used to bleed people. Later doctors decided that was a bad practice.

Today, new kinds of surgery are successful, but surgery can cause problems. Surgery can lead to a lack of blood flow or can cause blood clots to form. Leeches are good at helping blood flow and loosening blood clots. That's why doctors are starting to use them again.

Some people may put up **resistance** to the idea of using leeches on their body. However, doctors now realize that leeches can sometimes be more useful than drugs.

Leeches can suck blood and help wounds heal.

Today many animals are being used in amazing ways to help people. Even snakes can help people calm down when they get upset.

Snakes are also being used to predict earthquakes. Some people believe that before an earthquake occurs, snakes will move out of their nests. By watching the snakes, some scientists believe they can warn people that a severe earthquake is about to occur.

Snakes may be able to warn people about upcoming danger.

There are so many ways that animals can help people. One of the most common ways is by being pets. Pets make life more pleasant for their owners. They are good companions for people who live alone.

Animals can be hard workers and improve the lives of people. They can help people with disabilities, rescue people, heal them, and even warn them of danger. Animals are truly our best friends!

Glossary

ambition *n.* a strong desire to rise to a high position in life

infested *adj.* troubled or disturbed by large numbers of things, such as bugs

landslide *n.* the sliding of a mass of soil or rock down a steep slope

quicksand *n.* very deep, wet, soft sand that supports hardly any weight

resistance *n.* the act of striving against or opposing

rickety *adj.* likely to fall or break down; not sturdy

roamed *v.* wandered about with no special aim or plan

vast *adj.* very huge and wide; immense